MISSION STATEMENT: A NEW APPROACH TO STATE HISTORY

The Illinois Bicentennial is the perfect time to rethink our approach to teaching state history and *The Illinois Chronicles* is a tremendous resource to engage the natural curiosity of young learners.

CURIOSITY IS OUR MOST PRECIOUS NATURAL INSTINCT

Throughout history, in most schools, knowledge has been and is still traditionally chopped up into separate subjects (social studies, math, science, etc.) and then further divided into a timetable, syllabus, or curriculum at each grade level.

This is NOT the way the world naturally appears to a child. To a young mind everything is connected, and the real world is often far more fascinating than any story you can make up!

This is particularly the case when it comes to the precious sense of identity and place that young people gain as they progress through their school years prompting them to ask themselves, "Where do I fit in?"

This is why the Illinois Bicentennial really matters. This year we have a unique opportunity to rethink the way state history is taught—not just in social studies or at grade 4—but all the way through primary and secondary education and across all subject areas.

TIMELINES ARE A FABULOUS FRAMEWORK FOR LEARNING

I have been personally and professionally exploring this educational paradigm for over a decade and here's what I've learned. With a timeline, the arrangements of words and images allow children to explore cross-curricular knowledge through their own natural curiosity—starting wherever they like and making their own journeys through time without ever getting lost or losing context.

Using a timeline also means students can explore a wide spectrum of knowledge through their own interests be it sports, culture, politics, conflict, science, or personalities.

THE ILLINOIS CHRONICLES IS A PARADIGM SHIFT

It's a new way of looking at state history using a timeline and other content created for this very purpose. The timeline unfolds into a six-foot-long wallchart allowing simultaneous multiple users and creating an environment of discussion and debate. It takes readers on a journey through 100 key moments, from the foundation of Statehood in 1818 to the present day.

In addition to the timeline, *The Illinois Chronicles* features 50 "newspaper" articles, dramatically telling key moments from the State's history as if they happened yesterday. These articles provide a rich bed of content to support select events on the timeline. Finally, on the back of the timeline is a list of key places to visit, a summary of civic government, an honor roll of key figures, and a glossary.

Some historical accounts you and your students will already know, others will be new. Witness the moment of joy when a child discovers they know something their teachers or parents do not! That sense of discovery and joy at becoming an expert is just what I believe develops a love of learning.

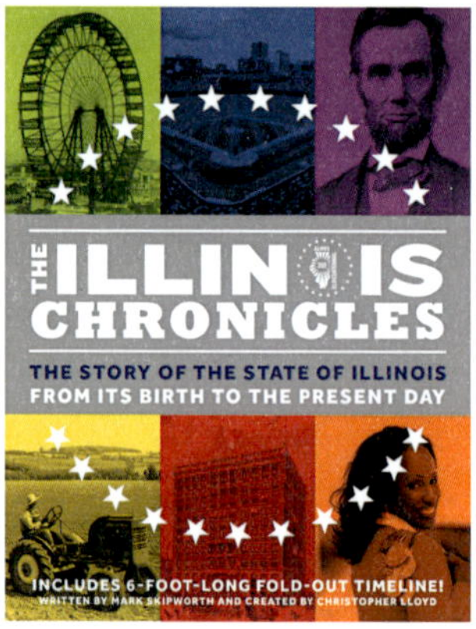

THE ILLINOIS CHRONICLES EDUCATOR'S GUIDE

In the following pages you will find a wide range of activities, ideas, and suggestions on how to use *The Illinois Chronicles* in the classroom to enhance the teaching of state history for grades K–12. This guide has been created in partnership with experts at the Illinois State Board of Education (ISBE) and carefully mapped to applicable state standards. Combined with intentional development and professional execution, we hope to infuse Illinois educators' lesson plans with high-interest activities and capture the instinctual curiosity of young learners.

Very best wishes for this special 200th birthday and the next 200 years to come!

Christopher Lloyd
World history author and CEO What on Earth Publishing

A MESSAGE FROM THE ILLINOIS STATE BOARD OF EDUCATION (ISBE)

The one-year celebration honoring Illinois' Bicentennial, which is December 3, 2018, has kicked off. There are many levels of involvement available during this year, including the opportunity to incorporate our State's rich history into classroom learning opportunities.

The Illinois Chronicles provide explanations of historical events as if they occurred today. The educator's guide provides Illinois' teachers with a variety of activity ideas that align with the articles found within *The Illinois Chronicles*. This guide is intended to be an idea-starter for ways to enhance the content within the classroom.

Each of the eight idea topics include activities aimed at different grade levels. A possible correlation between the Illinois Learning Standards and the various activities included are listed within each idea topic. The specific standards addressed from an activity may change, depending upon the nuances you adapt to make the activity your own. The ideas and activities listed in this guide are intended to provide entry points to a deeper investigation that fully addresses Illinois Learning Standards.

The Illinois Chronicles is being released to celebrate the Illinois Bicentennial, but the learning opportunities within the *Chronicles* and educator's guide can carry on well beyond the celebration year. The included events detail important contributions in history from Illinois and may be used as launching points for future learning for years to come. For example, consider using the article "Miraculous Moldy Melon" to begin an exploration of fungus and the development of antibiotics. Not only can this article lead to an inquiry into the scientific principles leading to the discovery of penicillin, but the historical implications can also be explored—how the course of World War II may have been altered without this contribution.

We encourage you to think outside the box and use the eight idea topics as launching points for inspired activities within the classroom!

1 BEHOLD! THE TIMELINE!

K–2 3–5 6–12

While many of the ideas we present in this resource correspond to specific articles or events in *The Illinois Chronicles*, we open our guide with general suggestions on introducing and using the timeline in the classroom. There are many points of entry into this engaging feature and we hope you discover some of your own along the way!

K–2

STANDARDS

ELA STANDARDS

K–2 Reading 1–3: Key ideas and details
K–2 Reading 7: Using illustrations to describe key ideas
K–2 Writing 2: Writing informational text
K–2 Writing 4–9: Produce and share information
K–2 Speaking and Listening 1: Collaborative conversations
K–2 Speaking and Listening 4–6: Presentation of knowledge and ideas

SOCIAL SCIENCE STANDARDS

SS.IS.3.K–2: Gather information from one or two sources with guidance and support from adults and/or peers.
SS.H.1.1: Create a chronological sequence of multiple events.
SS.H.2.1: Describe individuals and groups who have shaped a significant historical change.
SS.H.2.2: Compare individuals and groups who have shaped a significant historical change.

ACTIVITIES

- Choose six articles from *The Illinois Chronicles* (or events from the timeline) and read these articles aloud—perhaps at specified intervals, such as every Friday or every other day. After each article is read aloud, each student should create an illustration of the event (with a descriptive sentence or two, where able). After all six articles have been read, engage in a class discussion and ask the students to arrange their illustrations and descriptions of the six events in order, forming their own mini timelines. Students can share their timeline with a partner or in small groups before sharing with the whole class, practicing using ordinal terms.
- Shared Inquiry Extension: After completing their timeline, have the students choose their favorite event(s) to explore. Small groups of students can learn

more about a particular event using books or digital resources in a shared research project. The event or subject can be described or summarized in a drawing, written report, or other presentation form.

3–5

STANDARDS

ELA STANDARDS

3–5 Reading 1–3: Key ideas and details
3–5 Reading 7: Using illustrations to describe key ideas
3–5 Writing 2: Writing informational text
3–5 Writing 4–9: Produce and share information
3–5 Speaking and Listening 1: Collaborative conversations
3–5 Speaking and Listening 4–6: Presentation of knowledge and ideas

SOCIAL SCIENCE STANDARDS

SS.H.1.3: Create and use a chronological sequence of events.
SS.H.2.3: Describe how significant people, events, and developments have shaped their own community and region.
SS.H.3.4: Explain probable causes and effects of events and developments in Illinois history.
SS.H.1.5: Create and use a chronological sequence of related events to compare developments that happened at the same time.

ACTIVITIES

- My Timeline: Create an intergenerational timeline using events from three different generations (grandparent/senior, parent/adult, and events from your own life). Include three important or significant events that happened during each person's lifetime and plot on a timeline. (*Be sure to emphasize that if the student does not have access to information about other generations, they can interview neighbors, friends, or consider community resources like nursing homes, in order to allow all students the ability to interview adults and seniors.*) Find and add at least one event on the Illinois timeline that connects or adds value to your intergenerational timeline. Explore your trajectory and your role in history by predicting three significant or important events that will be a part of your future, and can be added to your timeline.
- Predict: What will Illinois look like in 2218, 200 years from now, in regard to the various categories color-coded on *The Illinois Chronicles* timeline (science, culture, sport, etc.)? What event(s) might you plot on a timeline marking notable changes within one or more of those categories? Write and/or draw about your prediction(s) and share with your classmates. Sort the class predictions into the appropriate color-coded categories. Additional connections can be made to the "My Timeline" activity above, by adding their predictions to their intergenerational timeline.

- Time Capsule: After exploring some key Illinois history events and figures, gather artifacts, objects, and symbols representing Illinois and place them in a time capsule. Imagine this time capsule will be opened in 200 years and you want future Illinois residents to know our history. Be sure to "make the case" for each object as space will be limited.

6–12

STANDARDS

ELA STANDARDS

6–12 RH and RI 1–3: Key ideas and details
6–12 RH and RI 7–9: Integration of knowledge and ideas
6–12 W and WHST 1 and 2: Writing argument and informative text
6–12 W and WHST 7–9: Research to build and present knowledge

SOCIAL SCIENCE STANDARDS

SS.H.1.6–8.LC: Classify series of historical events and developments as examples of change and/or continuity.
SS.H.1.6–8.MdC: Analyze connections among events and developments in broader historical contexts.
SS.H.2.6–8.MC: Analyze how people's perspectives influenced what information is available in the historical sources they created.
SS.H.3.6–8.MdC: Detect possible limitations in the historical record based on evidence collected from different kinds of historical sources.
SS.H.4.6–8.MC: Organize applicable evidence into a coherent argument about the past.
SS.H.1.9–12: Evaluate how historical developments were shaped by time and place as well as broader historical contexts.
SS.H.2.9–12: Analyze change and continuity within and across historical eras.
SS.H.8.9–12: Analyze key historical events and contributions of individuals through a variety of perspectives, including those of historically underrepresented groups.

ACTIVITIES

- What's Left Out?: Explore the timeline, research state history, and identify a major event in Illinois history that is not included in *The Illinois Chronicles* timeline. Make a case for WHY it should be included (or excluded), especially in the context of the events which are currently represented.
- Identify which events from *The Illinois Chronicles* timeline had ripple effects throughout the nation and/or the world. Find corresponding news articles from various perspectives (local, national, global) to make connections and note disparities between the way the event is presented in this account and in the articles found.

2 MOLDY MELON

K–5 6–12

"Moldy Mary" was so nicknamed for her contribution to the discovery of the miraculous mold removed from the rind of a cantaloupe, which was potent enough to mass produce penicillin, heralding the dawn of the age of antibiotics.

MASSACRE ON ST. VALENTINE'S DAY

Nuclear Age dawns

RAINBOW CITY, SHOWCASE FOR THE MODERN WORLD

MIRACULOUS MOLDY MELON

MEDICINE FROM ROTTEN FRUIT SET TO SAVE ALLIED LIVES

DATE: 1943

ARTICLE: "MIRACULOUS MOLDY MELON"

K–5

STANDARDS

SCIENCE STANDARDS

K-LS1-1: Use observations to describe patterns of what plants and animals (including humans) need to survive.

3-LS-1-1: Develop models to describe that organisms have unique and diverse life cycles but all have in common birth, growth, reproduction, and death.

5-LS2-1: Develop a model to describe the movement of matter among plants, animals, decomposers, and the environment.

SOCIAL SCIENCE STANDARDS

SS.H.1.1: Create a chronological sequence of multiple events.

SS.H.2.1: Describe individuals and groups who have shaped a significant historical change.

SS.H.1.3: Create and use a chronological sequence of events.

SS.H.1.5: Create and use a chronological sequence of related events to compare developments that happened at the same time.

SS.H.3.5: Explain probable causes and effects of events and developments in U.S. history.

ACTIVITIES

- Capture your students' imaginations with a controlled mold-growing experiment. Utilize existing lesson plans from reputable sources that use bread, fruit, and other readily-available materials. We recommend the EPA (Environmental Protection Agency) lesson plan called "Hold the Mold" for its coverage of this topic. The downloadable PDF guide they provide includes a "Student Mold Growth Observation Worksheet" to easily document student engagement.
- Research where in the natural world we find fungi, and the roles they play in food webs. Investigate why mushrooms so often appear near trees and on forest floors.

- Explore how fungi develop symbiotic and pathologic relationships with plants (mycorrhiza). How has this relationship affected life on earth, in particular, the colonization of life on land 400 million years ago?
- Analyze the potential good and the known harm molds cause as both hosts and toxins. What properties of fungus was the Department of Agriculture seeking as a catalyst for growing penicillin and how were samples procured and evaluated?
- Create a timeline of six key inventions or turning points that influenced the outcome of WWII, in addition to the development of antibiotics as a treatment for allied troops.
- Invite guest speakers to the classroom to explore modern careers related to how we grow and utilize fungi, as well as to explore initiatives in harnessing the power of fungi for potential problem-solving in health sciences and agriculture. Consider a cheesemaker, a mushroom farmer, or a mold remediation technician in addition to mycologists, toxicologists, and bacteriologists.

6–12

STANDARDS

SCIENCE STANDARDS

MS-LS1-1: Conduct an investigation to provide evidence that living things are made of cells, either one cell or many different numbers and types of cells.

MS-LS2-3: Develop a model to describe the cycling of matter and flow of energy among living and nonliving parts of an ecosystem.

HS-LS1-1: Construct an explanation based on evidence for how the structure of DNA determines the structure of proteins which carry out the essential functions of life through systems of specialized cells.

HS-LS2-3: Construct and revise an explanation based on evidence for the cycling of matter and flow of energy in aerobic and anaerobic conditions.

SOCIAL SCIENCE STANDARDS

SS.G2.6–8.MC: Evaluate how cultural and economic decisions influence environments and the daily lives of people in both nearby and distant places.

SS.H.1.6–8.MdC: Analyze connections among events and developments in broader historical contexts.

SS.H.4.6–8.MC: Organize applicable evidence into a coherent argument about the past.

SS.H.1.9–12: Evaluate how historical developments were shaped by time and place as well as broader historical contexts.

SS.H.4.9–12: Analyze how people and institutions have reacted to environmental, scientific, and technological changes.

SS.H.8.9–12: Analyze key historical events and contributions of individuals through a variety of perspectives, including those of historically underrepresented groups.

SS.H.11.9–12: Analyze multiple and complex causes and effects of events in the past.

ACTIVITIES

- Explore the research, development, and applied sciences of the U.S. Department of Agriculture, the Food and Drug Administration, the U.S. Military, and the pharmaceutical industry in producing penicillin and other fungus-based resources as tools for major health initiatives and military efforts.
- Why are antibiotics important? Predict what might have happened during WWII had antibiotics not existed. Evaluate the impact of antibiotics and how they have affected healthcare.
- Investigate how bacteria adapt to make antibiotics less or even ineffective over time. Research antibiotic resistant bacteria cases and discuss various outcomes. Speculate how this will influence the future of medicine and human health.
- Write a dystopian short story or letter to a friend describing a future where modern antibiotics have become ineffective against bacterial colonies of "superbugs".

3 ENGINEERING MARVELS

3–5 6–12

Chicago hosted two World's Fairs just 40 years apart. Both exhibitions featured technology displays and sights previously unseen, but which are still used today. The 1893 Columbian Exposition, or World's Fair, debuted Mr. Ferris's great wheel. The modern wheel on Chicago's Navy Pier, just a few miles from its debut location, pays homage to the original. The 1933 Century of Progress World's Fair brought to life "dream cars" and "homes of tomorrow" for thousands of visitors to this dynamic display of culture and technology, and homes throughout the world don features proposed in the "Rainbow City". In addition to the two themes suggested below, consider the many STEM-based articles in *The Illinois Chronicles* as a snapshot of 200 years of Illinois engineering marvels.

DATE: 1893, WORLD'S COLUMBIAN EXPOSITION
ARTICLE: "A MODERN WONDER OF THE WORLD"

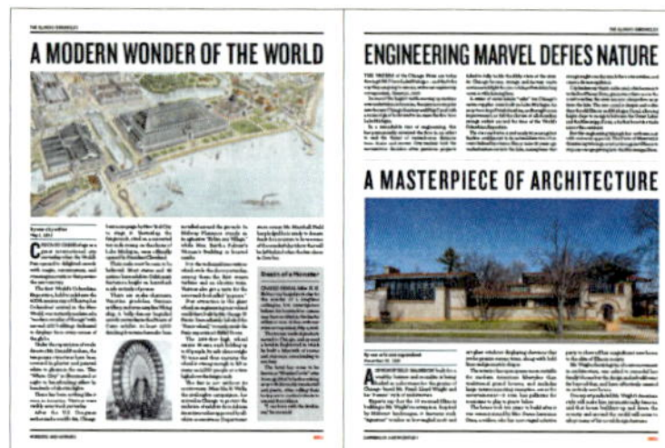
A MODERN WONDER OF THE WORLD

ENGINEERING MARVEL DEFIES NATURE

A MASTERPIECE OF ARCHITECTURE

3–5

SCIENCE STANDARDS

3–5-ETS1-1: Define a simple design problem reflecting a need or a want that includes specified criteria for success and constraints on materials, time, or cost.
3–5-ETS1-2: Generate and compare multiple possible solutions to a problem based on how well each is likely to meet the criteria and constraints of the problem.
3–5-ETS1-3: Plan and carry out fair tests in which variables are controlled and failure points are considered to identify aspects of a model or prototype that can be improved.

ACTIVITY

- Explore the engineering principles which formed the basis of the Ferris Wheel. How did Mr. Ferris engage in the design and engineering process? What trials and previous designs existed? How did he choose materials and what skills did his laborers need to execute his plan? Integrate the Arts: design a poster or advertisement encouraging fair-goers to give The Great Wheel a whirl!

DATE: 1933, A CENTURY OF PROGRESS WORLD'S FAIR
ARTICLE: "RAINBOW CITY, SHOWCASE FOR THE MODERN WORLD"

MASSACRE ON ST. VALENTINE'S DAY
RAINBOW CITY, SHOWCASE FOR THE MODERN WORLD
Nuclear Age dawns
MIRACULOUS MOLDY MELON
MEDICINE FROM ROTTEN FRUIT SET TO SAVE ALLIED LIVES

6–12

STANDARDS

SCIENCE STANDARDS

MS-ETS1-1: Define the criteria and constraints of a design problem with sufficient precision to ensure a successful solution, taking into account relevant scientific principles and potential impacts on people and the natural environment that may limit possible solutions.
MS-ETS1-2: Evaluate competing design solutions using a systematic process to determine how well they meet the criteria and constraints of the problem.
MS-ETS1-3: Analyze data from tests to determine similarities and differences among several design solutions to identify the best characteristics of each that can be combined into a new solution to better meet the criteria for success.
MS-ETS1-4: Develop a model to generate data for iterative testing and modification of a proposed object, tool, or process such that an optimal design can be achieved.

SOCIAL SCIENCE STANDARDS

SS.H.1.6–8.LC: Classify series of historical events and developments as examples of change and/or continuity.
SS.H.2.9–12: Analyze change and continuity within and across historical eras.
SS.H.6.9–12: Analyze the concept and pursuit of the American Dream.

ACTIVITIES

- Evaluate which technologies showcased at the fair came into use, which did not, and why? Do you know anyone with a personal helicopter pad, for instance?
- Explore what has changed about a particular device or tool from 1933 to today. For example, what features did Cadillac unveil in 1933 and what features are they advertising in commercials and at car shows today?
- If you were to design a home (or city) of the future, what features or inventions might you dare to dream and incorporate into your design? Consider all three major design principles—aesthetics, function, and innovation—in your proposal.
- Imagine you are the lead planner in designing the next Century of Progress World's Fair. Propose exhibits for the fair demonstrating forthcoming or new technologies.
- Invite guest speakers to illustrate how their company incorporates aesthetics, functions, and innovation into their product(s).

4 LAND OF LINCOLN

K–5 6–12

In the Land of Lincoln, you'll find this Presidential figure around every corner. From extensive academic resources to accessible site visits, Abraham Lincoln's physical presence in the State of Illinois presents dynamic opportunities for us to engage with this legendary figure.

DID YOU KNOW? The Abraham Lincoln Presidential Library and Museum offers an online collection of resources for teachers, including hands-on activities, vocabulary, research topics, critical thinking questions, and references to additional resources. Check out the website "Under His Hat" (http://underhishat.alplm.org/) for materials to accommodate classroom use at various grade levels.

DATE: 1858
ARTICLE: "'A HOUSE DIVIDED AGAINST ITSELF CANNOT STAND'"

"A HOUSE DIVIDED AGAINST ITSELF CANNOT STAND"

Mr. Lincoln's New Whiskers

TOMB RAIDERS FOILED

INFERNO LEAVES CHICAGO IN RUINS

HUNDREDS KILLED—MANY HOMES, CHURCHES, AND BUSINESSES DESTROYED

DATE: 1861
ARTICLE: "LINCOLN'S NEW WHISKERS"

DATE: 1944
ARTICLE: "WARTIME SPEECH FOR OUR TIMES"

WARTIME SPEECH FOR OUR TIMES

HIROSHIMA ATOM BOMB DROPPED BY QUINCY PILOT

Shining Temple to Tolerance Completed

A SIGHT TO SHAME AMERICA

K–5

STANDARDS

ELA STANDARDS

K–5 Reading 1–3: Key ideas and details
K–5 Reading 7: Using illustrations to describe key ideas
K–5 Writing 1 and 2: Writing opinion and informational text
K–5 Writing 4–9: Produce and share information
K–5 Speaking and Listening 1: Collaborative conversations
K–5 Speaking and Listening 4–6: Presentation of knowledge and ideas

SOCIAL SCIENCE STANDARDS

SS.CV.1.K: Describe roles and responsibilities of people in authority.
SS.H.1.K: Compare life in the past with life today.
SS.H.2.K: Explain the significance of our national holidays and the heroism and achievements of the people associated with them.
SS.H.2.1: Describe individuals and groups who have shaped a significant historical change.
SS.H.2.2: Compare individuals and groups who have shaped a significant historical change.

SS.H.2.3: Describe how significant people, events, and developments have shaped their own community and region.

SS.H.2.4: Using artifacts and primary sources, investigate how individuals contributed to the founding and development of Illinois.

ACTIVITIES

- It's All in a Hat: Use a Lincoln hat to collect or draw artifacts, objects, and symbols that represent moments in Illinois history, taking inspiration from the timeline. To do this, have students take turns identifying a moment from the timeline and identify the significance of that event or moment. Students should then select or draw an artifact, object, or symbol to represent the moment, which can be added to the hat. This could be done at regular intervals or on a schedule.
- Create a Lincoln Exhibition: While learning about the life and legacy of Abraham Lincoln, have students gather or create artifacts or symbols of his Presidency and use these as the basis for curating an exhibit on Lincoln. The exhibition may include text introductions to artifacts, verbal presentations, or living museum figures all coordinated to summarize why Lincoln is one of the most memorable Presidents of all time.
- Integrating the Arts: Abraham Lincoln had many nicknames before, during, and after his Presidency—among them were Honest Abe, The Great Emancipator, The Ancient One, and The Rail-Splitter. Determine what events or characteristics attributed to these nicknames and present your findings in an artistic rendering, such as a drawing, painting, cartoon, sculpture, avatar, or video.

6–12

STANDARDS

ELA STANDARDS

6–12 RH and RI 1–3: Key ideas and details

6–12 RH and RI 7–9: Integration of knowledge and ideas

6–12 W and WHST 1 and 2: Writing argument and informational text

6–12 W 3: Writing narrative text

6–12 W and WHST 7–9: Research to build and present knowledge

SOCIAL SCIENCE STANDARDS

SS.IS.8.6–8.MdC: Assess individual and collective capacities to take action to address problems and identify potential outcomes.

SS.H.4.6–8.MC: Organize applicable evidence into a coherent argument about the past.

SS.H.3.9–12: Evaluate the methods utilized by people and institutions to promote change.

SS.H.7.9–12: Identify the role of individuals, groups, and institutions in people's struggle for safety, freedom, equality, and justice.

ACTIVITIES

For older students, the complexity of Lincoln's speeches and character can be more fully explored. Here are a few starting points to begin discussing concepts of agency, authority, and identity.

- "Translate" a section of an historical speech into contemporary language.
- Adapt the Gettysburg Address, or portions of it, to present across social media platforms.
- Extract quotes from Lincoln's speeches to show how sound bites and info bites can be used in different contexts, by more than one party, and with divergent intentions.
- Study how Abraham Lincoln evolved politically throughout his life using primary sources, such as quotes and speeches, to note changes.
- Take a classroom vote on a controversial topic to identify a baseline. Write motivational speeches to convince your classmates to change their vote. Cast a second ballot following the presentations and evaluate what was effective in various speeches and why.
- Determine a topic which divides the country today and make suggestions on what type of leadership, actions, and persuasive techniques would be required to unite us. Present your own Plan of Action or draft your own "Gettysburg Address" to persuade the nation.

5 RESPONDING TO THE NEWS

K–5 6–8 9–12

Reading and responding to the news has long been a part of our cultural landscape and is closely tied to our understanding of the First Amendment. *The Illinois Chronicles* and timeline present dozens of opportunities to illustrate how we have historically responded to news and events, and how students today can take informed action in regard to topics across a 200-year continuum.

K–5

STANDARDS

ELA STANDARDS

K–5 Reading 1–3: Key ideas and details
K–5 Reading 7: Using illustrations to describe key ideas
K–5 Writing 1 and 2: Writing opinion and informational text
K–5 Writing 4–9: Produce and share information
K–5 Speaking and Listening 1: Collaborative conversations
K–5 Speaking and Listening 4–6: Presentation of knowledge and ideas

SOCIAL SCIENCE STANDARDS

SS.IS.4.K–2: Evaluate a source by distinguishing between fact and opinion.
SS.IS.5.K–2: Ask and answer questions about arguments and explanations.
SS.IS.4.3–5: Gather relevant information and distinguish between fact and opinion to determine credibility of multiple sources.
SS.IS.6.3–5: Construct and critique arguments and explanations using reasoning, examples, and details from multiple sources.

ACTIVITIES

- Choose an article in *The Illinois Chronicles* and highlight keywords and phrases. Use those words and phrases to summarize the article.
- Create a comic strip to comment on one of the news articles using three to five panels of artwork and/or dialogue.
- Create two columns on the board labeled "facts" and "opinions". Read an article aloud and pull out the sentences or ideas representing opinions, and those representing facts, and note them in the appropriate column.
- After reading aloud two or three articles, have the students discuss or write about which article they find the most important or impactful (or which had the biggest impact on people at the time). Ask them to include why they chose that article and what may have been different had the event never occurred.

- After learning about how newspapers include letters to the editor, respond to an event from the timeline as if you were alive during the event. Write a letter to the editor in response to the news including what you thought of that event and how it made you feel.

6–8

STANDARDS

ELA STANDARDS

6–8 RH and RI 1–3: Key ideas and details
6–8 RH and RI 7–9: Integration of knowledge and ideas
6–8 W and WHST 1 and 2: Writing argument and informational text
6–8 W and WHST 7–9: Research to build and present knowledge

SOCIAL SCIENCE STANDARDS

SS.IS.6.6–8.LC: Construct arguments using claims and evidence from multiple sources, while acknowledging their strengths and limitations.
SS.IS.6.6–8.MdC: Construct explanations using reasoning, correct sequence, examples, and details, while acknowledging their strengths and weaknesses.
SS.IS.8.6–8.LC: Analyze how a problem can manifest itself and the challenges and opportunities faced by those trying to address it.

ACTIVITIES

- *The Illinois Chronicles* presents a range of controversial issues. Respond to a single news article by writing a letter to the editor from an assigned perspective. For example, in the article "Illinois Women Win the Vote," students could be assigned to write from multiple perspectives such as a female suffragette, an opposition female, a male supporter, a male dissenter, a politician, or even as a business owner.
- Political cartoons and advertisements attempt to distill big ideas into a single image or short message. Create a political cartoon or ad on a topic presented in *The Illinois Chronicles* or timeline and note what considerations were made in addressing your topic.
- Choose an article from *The Illinois Chronicles* that may be controversial and offer a solution to the problems presented in the article. Create a sample social media feed informing others about this event and sharing your opinions with the world.

9–12

STANDARDS

ELA STANDARDS

9–12 RH and RI 1–3: Key ideas and details
9–12 RH and RI 7–9: Integration of knowledge and ideas

9–12 W and WHST 1 and 2: Writing argument and informational text
9–12 W and WHST 7–9: Research to build and present knowledge

SOCIAL SCIENCE STANDARDS

SS.IS.4.9–12: Gather and evaluate information from multiple sources while considering the origin, credibility, point of view, authority, structure, context, and corroborative value of the sources.

SS.IS.5.9–12: Identify evidence that draws information from multiple sources to revise or strengthen claims.

SS.IS.6.9–12: Construct and evaluate explanations and arguments using multiple sources and relevant, verified information.

SS.IS.7.9–12: Articulate explanations and arguments to a targeted audience in diverse settings.

SS.IS.8.9–12: Use interdisciplinary lenses to analyze the causes and effects of and identify solutions to local, regional, or global concerns.

ACTIVITIES

- Evaluate an article for its historical and contemporary effect on the immediate community, as well as through a broader lens (e.g. from a state, national, or global point of view). What concerns are the same at each level, and how do they change as each larger group is included in understanding the issue?
- Compare an article to the same topic as described in more recent news. Describe what actions have taken place since then and evaluate the motivations of the sources as described in perspective, context, authority, point of view, origin, structure, and context.
- Independently research a topic. Locate information which disagrees with the account in *The Illinois Chronicles* and compare the news as presented from alternate sources.
- Choose an event from *The Illinois Chronicles* or timeline and summarize how this issue has changed over time. Research individuals and organizations which have addressed this topic. Outline the current debate surrounding this subject and cite multiple sources to show contemporary differences in opinion and note why this issue is still newsworthy.

6 INVENTING IN ILLINOIS

K–5 9–12

Illinois has long been an incubator of inventions ranging from tools so commonplace as to now be considered rudimentary to one of the most dangerously bold energy advances in human history. For young learners, we recommend learning more about two Prairie State agricultural inventors who improved quality of life for generations. For older grades we hope to facilitate discussions focused on nuclear science, beginning with its birthplace in Illinois in 1942 through its impact on the world today and tomorrow.

FROM TOWN TO CITY IN JUST 4 YEARS

Mob Claims Life of Anti-Slavery Campaigner

ILLINOIS' OWN TRAIL OF TEARS

NEW HARVESTER BOOSTS FARMING

INGENIOUS HORSE-DRAWN REAPER CUTS, THRESHES, AND BALES ALL IN ONE GO

Religious Minority Forced To Flee Their Homes in Nauvoo

DATE: 1837–1851
ARTICLE: "NEW HARVESTER BOOSTS FARMING"

K–5

STANDARDS

SCIENCE STANDARDS

K–2-ETS1-1: Ask questions, make observations, and gather information about a situation people want to change to define a simple problem that can be solved through the development of a new or improved object or tool.

K–2-ETS1-2: Develop a simple sketch, drawing, or physical model to illustrate how the shape of an object helps it function as needed to solve a given problem.

K–2-ETS1-3: Analyze data from tests of two objects designed to solve the same problem to compare the strengths and weaknesses of how each performs.

3–5-ETS1-1: Define a simple design problem reflecting a need or a want that includes specified criteria for success and constraints on materials, time, or cost.

3–5-ETS1-2: Generate and compare multiple possible solutions to a problem based on how well each is likely to meet the criteria and constraints of the problem.

3–5-ETS1-3: Plan and carry out fair tests in which variables are controlled and failure points are considered to identify aspects of a model or prototype that can be improved.

SOCIAL SCIENCE STANDARDS

SS.H.1.K: Compare life in the past with life today.

SS.H.2.1: Describe individuals and groups who have shaped a significant historical change.

SS.H.2.2: Compare individuals and groups who have shaped a significant historical change.

SS.H.2.3: Describe how significant people, events, and developments have shaped their own community and region.

SS.H.3.4: Explain probable causes and effects of events and developments in Illinois history.

SS.H.3.5: Explain probable causes and effects of events and developments in U.S. history.

ACTIVITIES

- Explore the engineering successes of John Deere and Cyrus McCormick as two of Illinois's most dedicated inventors. Discuss how their contributions dramatically increased yields and cultivated Midwest prairies into the rich farmland that crisscrosses the State. Today, Illinois is a major producer of corn and soybeans, dozens of agricultural commodities, and even some specialty crops such as grapes, pumpkins, and Christmas trees.
- Mechanical Reaper: Have students try to gather and bundle objects such as straws or toothpicks with their hands. Afterward, try utilizing a variety of tools such as a brush, comb, scoop, etc., to see if they can improve upon the process. Connect this hands-on experience to the ease and efficiency with which the reaper allowed farmers to bundle wheat.
- Steel Plow: Discover why the steel plow was an improvement from the wooden one. Try digging in the ground outside with wooden tools (e.g. a wooden spoon) versus metal tools (e.g. a trowel). Discuss why steel was a stronger and more durable material, better suited to help farmers cut through the hard Illinois soil.
- "Shark Tank" Inventions of the Future: Have students think about an invention they believe would make life easier for individuals or businesses. After creating a concept, students can take their design (depending on time) through various phases of development and testing.

RECOMMENDED RESOURCES

- Online: Check out http://www.agintheclassroom.org/ for USDA Agriculture in the Classroom resources and materials.
- In print: Take a look at *John Deere, That's Who!*, a picture book biography by Tracy Nelson Maurer, published by Henry Holt & Company (2017).

DATE: 1942
ARTICLE: "NUCLEAR AGE DAWNS"

DATE: 1945
ARTICLE: "HIROSHIMA ATOM BOMB DROPPED BY QUINCY PILOT"

MASSACRE ON ST. VALENTINE'S DAY

Nuclear Age dawns

RAINBOW CITY, SHOWCASE FOR THE MODERN WORLD

MIRACULOUS MOLDY MELON

MEDICINE FROM ROTTEN FRUIT SET TO SAVE ALLIED LIVES

WARTIME SPEECH FOR OUR TIMES

YOUNGSTERS BUY A PIECE OF HISTORY TO INSPIRE LEADERS OF TODAY

Shining Temple to Tolerance Completed

A SIGHT TO SHAME AMERICA

HIROSHIMA ATOM BOMB DROPPED BY QUINCY PILOT

9–12

STANDARDS

SCIENCE STANDARDS

HS-ETS1-1: Analyze a major global challenge to specify qualitative and quantitative criteria and constraints for solutions that account for societal needs and wants.

HS-ETS1-2: Design a solution to a complex real-world problem by breaking it down into smaller, more manageable problems that can be solved through engineering.
HS-ETS1-3: Evaluate a solution to a complex real-world problem based on prioritized criteria and trade-offs that account for a range of constraints, including cost, safety, reliability, and aesthetics, as well as possible social, cultural, and environmental impacts.
HS-ETS1-4: Use a computer simulation to model the impact of proposed solutions to a complex real-world problem with numerous criteria and constraints on interactions within and between systems relevant to the problem.

SOCIAL SCIENCE STANDARDS

SS.H.1.9-12: Evaluate how historical developments were shaped by time and place as well as broader historical contexts.
SS.H.4.9-12: Analyze how people and institutions have reacted to environmental, scientific, and technological changes.
SS.H.5.9-12: Analyze the factors and historical context that influenced the perspectives of people during different historical eras.
SS.H.7.9-12: Identify the role of individuals, groups, and institutions in people's struggle for safety, freedom, equality, and justice.
SS.H.10.9-12: Analyze the causes and effects of global conflicts and economic crises.
SS.H.11.9-12: Analyze multiple and complex causes and effects of events in the past.
SS.H.12.9-12: Analyze the geographic and cultural forces that have resulted in conflict and cooperation.

ACTIVITIES

In addition to hosting the world's first nuclear reactor, Illinois is the home to two dedicated nuclear facilities, as well as the Atomic Science Bulletin. The historical relevance of these places and events combined with modern concerns and perspectives will foster meaningful discussion of the impact of nuclear science.

- Engage in historical and contemporary investigations of the Fermilab or the Argonne National Laboratory and consider each location for site visits and as opportunities to connect with nuclear scientists.
- Consider the benefits of nuclear energy against the dangers of nuclear proliferation and atomic warfare. Debate/discuss the merits of such advances and develop an ethics plan for managing nuclear science discoveries.
- Study the movement of the Atomic Scientists's Doomsday Clock and speculate what types of world events might move the clock forward or backward in time. Or, design your own "Doomsday Clock" and determine what events may influence the clock in the future.

7 HEROES OF ILLINOIS

K–5 6–12

Throughout the timeline and within the articles of *The Illinois Chronicles* we meet many noteworthy (and sometimes notorious) individuals. Here's an opportunity to explore the shining stars among the broad cast of characters in Illinois history. Roll out the red carpet! It's time for the...Oscars of Illinois!

K–5

STANDARDS

ELA STANDARDS

3–5 Reading 1–3: Key ideas and details
3–5 Reading 7: Using illustrations to describe key ideas
3–5 Writing 4–9: Produce and share information
3–5 Speaking and Listening 1: Collaborative conversations
3–5 Speaking and Listening 4–6: Presentation of knowledge and ideas

SOCIAL SCIENCE STANDARDS

SS.IS.8.3–5: Use listening, consensus building, and voting procedures to decide on and take action in their classroom and school.
SS.H.2.3: Describe how significant people, events, and developments have shaped their own community and region.
SS.CV.2.4: Explain how a democracy relies on people's responsible participation, and draw implications for how individuals should participate.
SS.CV.3.4: Identify core civic virtues (such as honesty, mutual respect, cooperation, and attentiveness to multiple perspectives) and democratic principles (such as equality, freedom, liberty, and respect for individual rights) that guide our State and nation.

OSCARS OF ILLINOIS ACTIVITY

- Have students nominate individuals from *The Illinois Chronicles* or timeline to form an "honor roll" of nominees and then campaign for those candidates using speeches, advertising, and other persuasive arts.
- Classify the nominees into the color-coded categories from the timeline and have students vote within each category. Students should defend their vote through written arguments, class discussions, cooperative learning, or debates.
- Once the winners have been chosen, ask students to present the awards in partners or groups, including writing and delivering acceptance speeches.

Tip: The Academy Awards (or Oscars) take place in the Spring each year. To align with this popular event, late February or early March can be a recommended target date for your very own "Awards Ceremony".

6–12

***The Illinois Chronicles* captures a range of historical events and figures. Consider heroes, villains, agitators, inciters, victims, and bystanders to gain a more complex understanding of Illinois's contributions to social justice and reform.**

STANDARDS

ELA STANDARDS

6–12 RH and RI 1–3: Key ideas and details
6–12 RH and RI 7–9: Integration of knowledge and ideas
6–12 W and WHST 7–9: Research to build and present knowledge

SOCIAL SCIENCE STANDARDS

SS.IS.8.6–8.LC: Analyze how a problem can manifest itself and the challenges and opportunities faced by those trying to address it.

SS.IS.8.6–8.MdC: Assess individual and collective capacities to take action to address problems and identify potential outcomes.

SS.IS.8.6–8.MC: Apply a range of deliberative and democratic procedures to make decisions and take action in schools and community contexts.

SS.H.1.6–8.MC: Use questions generated about individuals and groups to analyze why they, and the developments they shaped, are seen as historically significant.

SS.H.4.6–8.MC: Organize applicable evidence into a coherent argument about the past.

SS.IS.8.9–12: Use interdisciplinary lenses to analyze the causes and effects of and identify solutions to local, regional, or global concerns.

SS.IS.9.9–12: Use deliberative processes and apply democratic strategies and procedures to address local, regional, or global concerns and take action in or out of school.

SS.H.3.9–12: Evaluate the methods utilized by people and institutions to promote change.

SS.H.7.9–12: Identify the role of individuals, groups, and institutions in people's struggle for safety, freedom, equality, and justice.

ACTIVITIES

- Identify a social justice issue presented on the timeline. Use news events which have happened since to document how much progress we have (or have not) made, and speculate on some of the reasons why.
- Review the social justice issues addressed in *The Illinois Chronicles* and describe which have changed and identify if any are no longer controversial. As an extension, think about new issues that have arisen in your lifetime and predict which social justice issues might capture headlines in the future.
- What have we learned from the past based on social justice issues and how might YOU (as an individual) or ILLINOIS (as a state) make contributions? Look for community resources and groups which are currently working on a social justice issue and develop an action plan in moving the issue forward. Or, hold a mock community forum to discuss the issue across various interest groups.

8 HAPPY 200TH BIRTHDAY, ILLINOIS!

K–5 6–12

The ideas we have presented in this guide, combined with your diverse classroom experiences, preferred learning strategies, various disciplines, and personal creative concepts, are just what we need to make state history a dynamic and engaging area of study. We envision classrooms across the State delving into forgotten places and taking a deeper look at key figures and events throughout the school year. Consider the culmination of all these classroom explorations a celebration of our great State and your influence in creating leaders for the next 200 years!

K–5

STANDARDS

ELA STANDARDS

K–5 Writing 1 and 2: Writing opinion and informational text
K–5 Writing Standards 4–9: Produce and share information
K–5 Speaking and Listening 4–6: Presentation of knowledge and ideas

SOCIAL SCIENCE STANDARDS

SS.H.1.K: Compare life in the past with life today.

SS.H.2.K: Explain the significance of our national holidays and the heroism and achievements of the people associated with them.

SS.H.2.1: Describe individuals and groups who have shaped a significant historical change.

SS.G.1.2: Construct and interpret maps and other graphic representations of both familiar and unfamiliar places.

SS.H.2.2: Compare individuals and groups who have shaped a significant historical change.

SS.H.2.3: Describe how significant people, events, and developments have shaped their own community and region.

SS.G.1.4: Construct and interpret maps of Illinois and the United States using various media.

SS.G.2.4: Analyze how the cultural and environmental characteristics of places in Illinois change over time.

ACTIVITIES

Create a birthday party atmosphere and celebrate our State with everything from facts and figures to cake and ice cream! Invite community members to engage in the celebration and learn more about the events students have explored.

- Invite key characters from *The Illinois Chronicles*, have students dress up or role play those characters and present their role in state history.
- Make a cake in the shape of our State and decorate it with symbols of our legacy.
- Create an oversized map of Illinois and highlight places of significance throughout the State as referenced in *The Illinois Chronicles* articles or timeline. Indicate the places on the map where the events took place with an image or symbol to represent the event or its significance. Be sure to include not only the locations highlighted on the back of the timeline but track other events discussed in your study of Illinois!
- Create bunting or garland decorations using key moments from the timeline on each individual flag. On one side put an image to commemorate that moment and on the other a brief description of the event and its significance. Complete and hang the bunting up in time for the day of the birthday party.
- Ask students to work in groups to summarize the six subject-area themes from the timeline (sport and adventure, conflict and tragedy, science and engineering, commerce and architecture, culture and heritage, and politics and civil rights). The groups can then create a presentation or dramatic representation that showcases the importance of those events.
- Have students create a multiple-choice quiz of 10 or so events from Illinois history. Encourage them to quiz their classmates, teachers, and parents/adults, and graph the results for display at the party. For quick reference, make sure a copy of the *The Illinois Chronicles* timeline is readily accessible—or even mounted on the classroom wall. As an added bonus, if community members join the party, test their knowledge about Illinois history, too!

6–12

STANDARDS

ELA STANDARDS

6–12 RH and RI 1–3: Key ideas and details
6–12 RH and RI 7–9: Integration of knowledge and ideas
6–12 W and WHST 1 and 2: Writing argument and informational text
6–12 W and WHST 7–9: Research to build and present knowledge

SOCIAL SCIENCE STANDARDS

SS.H.1.6–8.MdC: Analyze connections among events and developments in broader historical contexts.

SS.H.8.9–12: Analyze key historical events and contributions of individuals through a variety of perspectives, including those of historically underrepresented groups.